WHAT *Is the* TRINITY?

The Crucial Questions Series By R.C. Sproul

Who *Is* Jesus?

Can I Trust *the* Bible?

Does *Prayer* Change Things?

Can I *Know* God's Will?

How Should I *Live* in This World?

What Does It Mean *to Be* Born Again?

Can I Be Sure *I'm* Saved?

What *Is* Faith?

What Can I *Do with* My Guilt?

What *Is the* Trinity?

What *Is* Baptism?

Can I Have *Joy* in My Life?

Who Is *the* Holy Spirit?

Does God *Control* Everything?

How Can I Develop a Christian Conscience?

What *Is the* Lord's Supper?

What Is *the* Church?

What *Is* Repentance?

What Is *the Relationship between* Church *and* State?

Are These *the* Last Days?

What *Is the* Great Commission?

Can I *Lose My* Salvation?

Free digital editions available at ReformationTrust.com/FreeCQ

CRUCIAL
QUESTIONS
No. | 10

WHAT *Is the* TRINITY?

R.C. SPROUL

ℝ *Reformation Trust*   A DIVISION OF LIGONIER MINISTRIES, ORLANDO, FL

What Is the Trinity?

© 2011 by R.C. Sproul

Published by Reformation Trust Publishing
a division of Ligonier Ministries
421 Ligonier Court, Sanford, FL 32771
Ligonier.org   ReformationTrust.com

Printed in North Mankato, MN
Corporate Graphics
August 2015
First edition, eighth printing

Cover design: Gearbox Studios
Interior design and typeset: Katherine Lloyd, The DESK

Library of Congress Cataloging-in-Publication Data

Sproul, R. C. (Robert Charles), 1939-
  What is the trinity? / R. C. Sproul.
    p. cm. -- (The crucial questions series)
  Includes bibliographical references.
  ISBN 978-1-56769-259-4
  1. Trinity. I. Title.
  BT111.3.S86 2011
  231'.044--dc23

                                        2011019615

Contents

Chapter One

MONOTHEISM

The concept of the Trinity has emerged as a touchstone of truth, a non-negotiable article of Christian orthodoxy. However, it has been a source of controversy throughout church history, and there remains much confusion about it to this day, with many people misunderstanding it in very serious ways.

Some people think that the doctrine of the Trinity means that Christians believe in three gods. This is the idea of tritheism, which the church has categorically rejected throughout its history. Others see the Trinity as the church's retreat into contradiction. For instance, I once had a conversation with a man who had a PhD in philosophy, and he objected to Christianity on the grounds that the doctrine of the Trinity represented a manifest contradiction—the idea that one can also be three—at the heart of the Christian faith. Apparently this professor of philosophy was not familiar with the law of non-contradiction. That law states, "A cannot be A and non-A at the same time and in the same relationship." When we confess our faith in the Trinity, we affirm that God is one in essence and three in person. Thus, God is one in A and three in B. If we said that He is one in essence and three in essence, that would be a contradiction. If we said He is one in person and three in person, that also would be a contradiction. But as mysterious as the Trinity is, perhaps even above and beyond our capacity to understand it in its fullness, the historic formula is not a contradiction.

Before we can talk about the Trinity, we have to talk about unity, because the word *Trinity* means "tri-unity." Behind the concept of unity is the biblical affirmation of monotheism. The prefix *mono* means "one or single," while the root word *theism* has to do with God. So, *monotheism* conveys the idea that there is only one God.

THE EVOLUTION OF RELIGIONS

The issue of whether the Bible is uniformly monotheistic came into question in the fields of religion and philosophy during the nineteenth century. One of the most dominant philosophers of the nineteenth century was Friedrich Hegel. He developed a complex and speculative philosophy of history that had at its core a concept of historical development or evolution. In the nineteenth century, thinkers were preoccupied with the concept of evolution, but not simply with respect to biology. *Evolution* became almost a buzzword in the academic world and in the scientific community, and it was applied not only to the development of living things, but also to political institutions. For instance, so-called social Darwinism understood human history as the progress of civilizations.

Hegel's followers also applied these evolutionary ideas to the development of religious concepts. They worked with this assumption: All spheres of creation, including religion, follow the pattern of evolution we see in the biological realm, which is evolution from the simple to the complex. In the case of religion, this means that all developed religions evolved from the simple form of animism.

The term *animism* denotes the idea that there are living souls, spirits, or personalities in what we would normally understand to be inanimate or non-living objects, such as rocks, trees, totem poles, statues, and so on.

The idea that primitive religion was animistic seemed to be confirmed by scholars who examined primitive cultures that had survived to the present. Scholars who went to the remote corners of the world and studied the religions of these cultures found that they contained strong elements of animism. So, the assumption was accepted that all religions begin with animism and progressively evolve.

Some scholars believed that animism could be found in the earliest pages of the Old Testament. They often cited the account of the fall, for Adam and Eve were tempted by a serpent that assumed personal characteristics (Gen. 3). He could reason, speak, and act with volition. Critics also referred to the experience of Balaam, whose donkey was enabled to speak (Num. 22). They said this showed that the biblical writers believed there was a spirit in the donkey, just like there was a spirit in the serpent. When I was in seminary, I heard a professor say that animism was being practiced when Abraham met the angels by the oaks of Mamre (Gen. 18). The professor said that Abraham was really conversing with the gods in the trees. However, there is not a shred of evidence in the text that Abraham was engaged in any kind of animism.

Those who hold to an evolutionary view of religion say that the next step in the process is polytheism: many gods. Polytheism was common in the cultures of antiquity. The Greek religion, the Roman religion, the Norse religion, and many others had a god or a goddess for almost every human function: a god of fertility, a god of wisdom, a god of beauty, a god of war, and so on. We're all familiar with this idea from our studies of the mythologies of the ancient world. Simply put, people believed that many gods existed to serve various functions of human life.

After polytheism, the next stage of religious development is called henotheism, which is a sort of hybrid between polytheism and monotheism, a transitional stage, as it were. Henotheism is belief in one god (the prefix *hen* comes from a Greek word for "one," a different word from *mono*), but the idea is that there is one god for each people or nation, and each one reigns over a particular geographical area. For example, henotheism would hold that there was a god for the Jewish people (Yahweh), a god for the Philistines (Dagon), a god for the Canaanites (Baal), and so on. However, this view does not posit that there was only one god ultimately.

Henotheistic peoples recognized that other nations had their own gods, and they often saw battles between nations as battles between the gods of the peoples. Some scholars find this idea in the Old Testament because many of the conflicts recorded there are cast as the God of Israel going up against Dagon, Baal, or another pagan god, but that does not mean Israel was henotheistic.

THE BIBLE: MONOTHEISTIC FROM THE OUTSET

Assuming this evolutionary framework, the nineteenth-century critics challenged the idea that the Bible is consistently monotheistic. There was an ongoing debate as to when monotheism began in Israel. The more conservative of these critics said there were hints of it at the time of Abraham. Others said that monotheism did not begin until the time of Moses. Some even rejected the idea that Moses was a monotheist, saying that monotheism did not begin until the time of the prophets, such as Isaiah around the eighth century BC. A few were even more skeptical, arguing that monotheism did not begin until after the Israelite exile in Babylon, making it a rather recent development in Jewish religion. So, orthodox scholarship has had to battle for the past hundred-plus years to defend the idea of the unity of God in Scripture.

Orthodox arguments hold that monotheism was present at the very beginning of biblical history. We read in the very first verse of Scripture, "In the beginning, God created the heavens and the earth." The creation narrative affirms that the God who is introduced on the first page of the Pentateuch has the entire creation as His domain, not just the limited geographical boundaries of Old Testament Israel. God is sovereign over heaven and earth, having made them at the word of His command.

Critics often note that in the early chapters of Scripture, there is a vacillation between two names for God. On the one hand, God is referred to as Jehovah or Yahweh; on the other hand, He is called Elohim. That name, Elohim, is striking because the suffix, *him*, is the plural ending of the Hebrew noun, so one could translate the name Elohim as "gods." However, while the name Elohim has a plural ending, it always appears with singular verb forms. So the writer was saying something that could not be interpreted to mean "many gods." Plus, as I noted above, God is revealed to us in the opening chapters of Genesis as the one who is sovereign over all things. So I think that those who hold that the name Elohim hints at polytheism are jumping to an incorrect conclusion.

When we come to Exodus 20, the account of the giving of the law, we see that the first commandment God gave on Sinai was strongly monotheistic. God said, "You shall have no other gods before me" (v. 3). Some would say this verse gives evidence of henotheism, because God is implying there *are* other gods, and the commandment is declaring that the people must not let those other gods outrank Him; He must be the chief deity in their lives. But the Hebrew indicates that when God says "before me," He is saying, "In My presence." His presence, of course, is ubiquitous; He is omnipresent. So when God says, "You shall have no other gods before me," He basically is saying that when a person worships anything apart from Him, whether that person lives in Israel, Canaan, Philistia, or anywhere else, he engages in an act of idolatry, because there is only one God. The second commandment therefore reinforces the first with its blanket prohibition of all forms of idolatry.

Later in the Pentateuch, we find a striking statement of monotheism. It appears in the *Shema*, ancient Israel's confession of its belief in one God: "Hear, O Israel: The LORD our God, the LORD is one" (Deut. 6:4).

In the prophetic books, we see an almost constant diatribe against the false gods of other religions. These gods are seen not as competing deities but as useless idols. In fact, the prophets characteristically make fun of people who worship trees, statues, and other things they have made with their own hands, as if a block of wood could be inhabited by an intelligent being. They ridicule the ideas of animism and polytheism consistently.

These affirmations of monotheism are a startling dimension of Old Testament faith because of the rarity of such assertions in the ancient world. Most of the cultures of antiquity from which we have historical records were not monotheistic. Some have argued that the Egyptians were the first monotheists because of their worship of Ra, the sun god, but there is a uniqueness in the monotheism that was native to Old Testament faith. The idea that there is one God was firmly established in the religion of Israel from the earliest pages of the Old Testament.

IF GOD IS ONE, HOW CAN HE BE THREE?

It is precisely because of this clear teaching of monotheism that the doctrine of the Trinity is so problematic. When we come to the New Testament, we find the church affirming the notion of monotheism, but also declaring that God the Father is divine, God the Son is divine, and God the Holy Spirit is divine. We have to understand that the distinctions in the Godhead do not refer to His essence; they do not refer to a fragmentation or compartmentalization of the very being of God.

How, then, can we maintain the Old Testament doctrine of monotheism in light of the clear New Testament affirmation of the triune character of the biblical God? Augustine once wrote, "The New [Testament] is in the Old [Testament] concealed; the Old is in the New revealed." To understand how the doctrine of the Trinity came to be such an important article of the Christian faith, we need to see that there was a development of the church's understanding of the nature of God based on the Scriptures. When we look into the Scriptures, we see what we call in theology "progressive revelation." This is the idea that, as time goes by, God unfolds more and more of His plan of redemption. He gives more and more of His self-disclosure by means of revelation. The fact that there is this progress in revelation does not mean that what God reveals in the Old Testament He then contradicts in the New Testament. Progressive revelation is not a corrective, whereby the latest unveiling from God rectifies a previous mistaken revelation. Rather, new revelation builds on what was given in the past, expanding what God has made known.

Therefore, we do not see a manifest teaching of God's triune nature on the first page of Scripture. There are hints of it very early in the Old Testament, but we do not have full information about the Trinitarian character of God in the Old Testament. That information comes later, in the New Testament, so we have to trace the development of this doctrine throughout redemptive history to see what the Bible is actually saying about these things.

Chapter Two

THE BIBLICAL WITNESS

One of the key issues the ancient Greek philosophers tried to resolve was the problem of "the one and the many." Much of early Greek philosophy was dedicated to this difficulty. How, the philosophers wondered, can we make sense out of so many diverse things that are part of our experience? Do we live in a universe that is ultimately coherent or ultimately chaotic? Science, for example, assumes that in order for us to have knowledge, there has to be coherence, some kind of order to things. So, our enterprise of scientific investigation presupposes what Carl Sagan called "cosmos," not chaos. This means that there must be something that gives unity to all of the diversity that we experience in the universe. In fact, the very word *universe* combines the concepts of unity and diversity—it describes a place of great diversity that nevertheless has unity.

The Greek philosophers sought to find the source of both unity and diversity in a coherent way. In my opinion, they never succeeded. But in the Christian faith, all diversity finds its ultimate unity in God Himself, and it is significant that even in God's own being we find both unity and diversity—in fact, in Him we find the ultimate ground for unity and diversity. In Him we find one being in three persons.

Unlike the Greeks, we have a source of authority for our beliefs in this sphere—the Scriptures. In this chapter, I want to give a brief overview of the biblical teaching on the Trinity, beginning with the Old Testament and, following the pattern of unfolding revelation, concluding with the New Testament.

SCATTERED HINTS IN THE OLD TESTAMENT

Even though we cannot find an explicit definition of the Trinity in the Old Testament, we do find scattered hints there about God's triune nature. We touched on one of those hints in chapter one—the name of God that appears in plural form, Elohim. The critics see the use of that name as an indication of a crass form of polytheism. Others, however, have seen in that plural name, particularly since it is accompanied by a singular verb, a cryptic reference to the plural character of God.

I do not think the name Elohim necessarily points to the Trinity. It could simply be a literary form similar to what we call the editorial plural or the editorial "we," which a writer or speaker uses to communicate a point. This device is often used by dignitaries; a king, a pope, or another person in high office prefaces his or her comments by saying, "We decree" or "We declare," even though the person is speaking only for himself or herself. More specifically, there is a Hebrew literary device called the plural of intensity, which calls attention to the depth of the character of God, in whom resides all elements of deity and majesty. So, I believe that the name Elohim is compatible with the doctrine of the Trinity and may be hinting in that direction, but the name itself does not demand that we infer that God is triune in His nature.

There are other significant hints about the Trinity in the Old Testament. It is also in the creation account that we first encounter the Spirit of God (Gen. 1:2). By bringing something out of nothing, the Spirit meets one of the criteria for deity that are set forth in the New Testament. That is another hint as to the multipersonal character of God early on in the Scriptures.

Another is found in the Old Testament passage that is quoted in the New Testament more often than any other text—Psalm 110. This psalm has a very strange beginning. The psalmist says, "The LORD says to my Lord: 'Sit at my right hand, until I make your enemies your footstool'" (v. 1). Characteristically, when we see the personal name of God, Yahweh, in the Old Testament, we also see His chief or supreme title, Adonai, associated with it. For instance, Psalm 8 says, "O LORD, our Lord, how majestic is your name in all the earth!" (v. 1a). In the Hebrew, "O LORD, our Lord" reads "O Yahweh, our Adonai"; there is a clear connection between Yahweh and Adonai. In Psalm 110, however, God is having a conversation with David's Lord: "The LORD [Yahweh] says to my Lord [Adonai]: Sit at my right hand. . . ." The New Testament picks up on this and talks about Jesus simultaneously being David's son *and* David's Lord. This psalm also provides another hint to the multiple dimensions of the being of God when it declares that God's Son will be a priest forever, an eternal priest after the order of Melchizedek (v. 4).

MONOTHEISM ASSUMED IN THE NEW TESTAMENT

When we come to the New Testament, we find that the concepts of monotheism that are so firmly established in the Old Testament are not only assumed, they are repeated again and again. Let me mention a couple of examples.

Acts 17 records the apostle Paul's address to the philosophers at the Areopagus in the ancient Greek city of Athens. We read: "So Paul, standing in the midst of the Areopagus, said: 'Men of Athens, I perceive that in every way you are very religious. For as I passed along and observed the objects of your worship, I found also an altar with this inscription, 'To the unknown god'"" (vv. 22–23a). When Paul came to Athens, he noticed that the city was given over to idolatry. He passed by numerous temples and saw religious activity everywhere. He even noticed, as if the Greeks were afraid they might leave one deity out, that they had an altar with this inscription: "To the unknown god." As he saw all this, his spirit was moved within him (v. 16); in other words, he was troubled about the abundance of false religion.

One of the most striking things that I encountered during my graduate work in the 1960s was the evidence that was emerging from the work of theological anthropologists and sociologists who were examining the religious views of various primitive tribes in the world. They were finding that while animism was outwardly prevalent in those cultures, the people frequently spoke about a god on the other side of the mountain or a god who was distantly removed from them. In other words, they had a concept of a high god who was not at the center of their daily religious practices. This god was like the unknown god of the Greeks, a god with whom they were not in contact but who nevertheless was there.

This concept conforms to Paul's declaration in Romans 1 that the God of all the universe has manifested Himself to everyone (vv. 18–20). That means that every human being knows of the existence of the Most High God, but the sinful character of humanity is such that all of us repress and bury that knowledge, and choose idols instead. That is why we are all held guilty before God.

Paul picked up on the Greeks' altar to the unknown god and said:

"What therefore you worship as unknown, this I proclaim to you. The God who made the world and everything in it, being Lord of heaven and earth, does not live in temples made by man, nor is he served by human hands, as though he needed anything, since he himself gives to all mankind life and breath and everything. And he made from one man every nation of mankind to live on all the face of the earth, having determined allotted periods and the boundaries of their dwelling place, that they should seek God, in the hope that they might feel their way toward him and find him. Yet he is actually not far from each one of us, for 'In him we live and move and have our being'; as even some of your own poets have said, 'For we are indeed his offspring.' Being then God's offspring, we ought not to think that the divine being is like gold or silver or stone, an image formed by the art and imagination of man. The times of ignorance God overlooked, but now he commands all people everywhere to repent, because he has fixed a day on which he will judge the world in righteousness by a man whom he has appointed; and of this he has given assurance to all by raising him from the dead." (vv. 23b–31)

Here Paul affirms the bedrock tenets of classical Jewish monotheism—one God who made all things and from whom everything derives.

INDICATIONS OF GOD'S TRI-UNITY

In 1 Corinthians 8, Paul again affirms the oneness of God, but he brings in a new element. In the midst of a discussion of the issue of eating food items that had been offered to idols, a pastoral problem that came up in the Corinthian church, Paul says:

Now concerning food offered to idols: we know that "all of us possess knowledge." This "knowledge" puffs up, but love builds up. If anyone imagines that he knows something, he does not yet know as he ought to know. But if anyone loves God, he is known by God. Therefore, as to the eating of food offered to idols, we know that "an idol has no real existence," and that "there is no God but one." For although there may be so-called gods in heaven or on earth—as indeed there are many "gods" and many "lords"—yet for us there is one God, the Father, from whom are all things and for whom we exist, and one Lord, Jesus Christ, through whom are all things and through whom we exist. (vv. 1–6)

The new element here is that Paul ascribes deity to Christ. He distinguishes between the Father and the Son, and he notes that all things are "from" the Father and "through" Christ, and that we exist "for" the Father and "through" the Son. Clearly, Paul is equating the Father and the Son in terms of Their divinity.

There are many passages in the New Testament that ascribe deity to Christ and to the Holy Spirit, more than I could cite in this chapter or indeed in this entire booklet. Still, let me reference a few of these passages to make the point that this teaching is present in the New Testament and that it is not obscure.

In John's gospel, Jesus makes a number of "I am" statements: "I am the bread of life" (6:48), "I am the door" (10:7), "I am the way, and the truth, and the life" (14:6), and others. In each of these statements, the wording in the Greek New Testament for "I am" is *ego eimi.* These Greek words also happen to be the words with which the essential name of God, Yahweh, is translated from the Hebrew. Jesus, then, by using this construction for Himself, is equating Himself with God.

There is another "I am" statement in John 8. Abraham was the great patriarch of Israel, the father of the faithful, who was deeply venerated by the Jewish community of Jesus' day. Jesus told the Jewish leaders that Abraham had rejoiced to see His day (v. 56). When the leaders asked how Jesus could possibly have seen Abraham, He replied, "Before Abraham was, I am" (v. 58). He did not say, "Before Abraham was, I was." Rather, He said, "I am." In doing so, He made a claim to eternity and deity. What many people miss in our day, the first-century contemporaries of Jesus caught rather quickly. They were filled with fury against Jesus because He, a mere man in their eyes, made Himself equal with God.

John's gospel also records the intriguing narrative of a post-resurrection appearance of Jesus. Some of His disciples had seen Him when Thomas was absent. When Thomas heard about it, he said, "Unless I see in his hands the mark of the nails, and place my finger in the mark of the nails, and place my hand into his side, I will never believe" (20:25). In the midst of this skepticism, Jesus appeared to him and offered His hands and His side (v. 27). John does not tell us whether Thomas ever actually probed Jesus' wounds, but he does say Thomas fell on his knees and cried out, "My Lord and my God!" (v. 28). That is significant. In the book of Acts, we are told that people on one occasion were so amazed by a miraculous healing that they wanted to worship Paul and Barnabas, but they rebuked the people immediately (14:11–15). Elsewhere in Scripture, when people see the manifestation of angels and begin to worship them, the angels prevent them, saying that they are not to be worshiped because they are creatures. But Jesus accepted Thomas' worship without rebuke. He recognized Thomas' confession as valid.

THE TRINITY CLEARLY AFFIRMED

The clearest reference to Jesus' deity in the New Testament comes at the opening of John's gospel. It reads, "In the beginning was the Word [that is, the *Logos*], and the Word was with God, and the Word was God" (1:1). In that first sentence, we see the mystery of the Trinity, because the *Logos* is said to have been with God from the beginning. There are different terms in the Greek language that can be translated by the English word *with*, but the word that is used here suggests the closest possible relationship, virtually a face-to-face relationship. Nevertheless, John makes a distinction between the *Logos* and God. God and the *Logos* are together, but they are not the same.

Then John declares that the *Logos* not only was *with* God, He *was* God. So in one sense, the Word must be distinguished from God, and in another sense, the Word must be identified with God.

The apostle says more. He adds: "He was in the beginning with God. All things were made through him, and without him was not any thing made that was made. In him was life, and the life was the light of men" (vv. 2–4).

Here we see eternality, creative power, and self-existence attributed to the *Logos*, who is Jesus.

The New Testament also states that the Holy Spirit is divine. We see this, for instance, in Jesus' triune formula for baptism. By the command of Christ, people are to be baptized in the name of the Father, of the Son, and of the Holy Spirit (Matt. 28:19). Likewise, Paul's closing benediction in his second letter to the Corinthians reads, "The grace of the Lord Jesus Christ and the love of God and the fellowship of the Holy Spirit be with you all" (13:14). The apostles also speak of the Father, Son, and Spirit cooperating to redeem a people for Themselves (2 Thess. 2:13–14; 1 Peter 1:2).

In these and many other passages in the New Testament, the deity of the Father, the Son, and the Holy Spirit is set forth explicitly or implicitly. When considered together with the Bible's clear teaching as to the oneness of God, the only conclusion is that there is one God in three persons—the doctrine of the Trinity.

Chapter Three

CONTROVERSIES IN
THE EARLY CHURCH

When I was doing my doctoral studies in Holland, Professor G. C. Berkouwer gave a yearlong series of lectures on the history of heresy. It was an extremely valuable course because one of the best ways of learning orthodoxy is by learning what is false. In fact, heresy historically has forced the church to be precise, to define its doctrines and differentiate truth from falsehood. The early years of the church produced numerous heresies with regard to the persons of the Godhead, and those errors pushed the church to refine its understanding of the Trinity.

Nearly every Christian community in the world today affirms the assertions of the so-called ecumenical councils of church history, the two chief of which were the Council of Nicea in the fourth century and the Council of Chalcedon in the fifth century. It is worthwhile to familiarize ourselves with the controversies that provoked those councils, for they were intimately concerned with the nature of the persons of the Godhead. The overriding question had to do with how the biblical concept of monotheism could be reconciled with the biblical affirmations of the deity of Christ particularly, but also of the Holy Spirit.

In the previous chapter, we looked at the prologue of John's gospel, where the apostle speaks of the Word (the *Logos*), who was in the beginning, who was with God, and who was Himself God. The concept of the *Logos* was a major preoccupation of the Christian church in the first three centuries. A number of church leaders focused on the *Logos* as a second divine person of the Godhead. These scholars clearly were moving in the direction of the doctrine of the Trinity. Others, however, were zealous to defend the idea of God's oneness. That led to the development of a number of theological propositions that later were deemed heretical. Those errors forced the church to define its understanding of the Trinity in an official way.

MODALISM AND ADOPTIONISM

One of the first of these heretical movements that emerged in the third and fourth centuries was monarchianism. Few people are acquainted with this theological term, but the root word is quite familiar: *monarch*. When we think about a monarch, we think of a ruler of a nation, a king or a queen. If we break down the word *monarch*, we find that it consists of a prefix, *mono*, which means "one," coupled with the word *arch*, which comes from the Greek *arche*. This word could mean "beginning"; for instance, it appears in the prologue of John's gospel, when the apostle writes, "In the beginning was the Word." But it also could mean "chief or ruler." So, a monarch was a single ruler, and a monarchy was a system of rule by one. Monarchianism, then, was the attempt to preserve the unity of God, or monotheism.

The first great heresy that the church had to confront with respect to monarchianism was called "modalistic monarchianism" or simply "modalism." The idea behind modalism was that all three persons of the Trinity are the same person, but that they behave in unique "modes" at different times. Modalists held that God was initially the Creator, then became the Redeemer, then became the Spirit at Pentecost. The divine person who came to earth as the incarnate Jesus was the same person who had created all things. When He returned to heaven, He took up His role as the Father again, but then returned to earth as the Holy Spirit. As you can see, the idea here was that there is only one God, but that He acts in different modes, or different expressions, from time to time.

The chief proponent of modalism was a man named Sabellius. According to one ancient writer, Sabellius illustrated modalism by comparing God to the sun. He noted that the sun has three modes: its form in the sky, its light, and its warmth. By way of analogy, he said, God has various modes: the form corresponds to the Father, the light is the Son, and the warmth is the Spirit.

A second form of monarchianism that appeared was called "dynamic monarchianism" or "adoptionism." This school of thought was also committed to preserving monotheism, but its adherents wanted to give honor and central importance to the person of Christ. Those who propagated this view held that at the time of creation, the first thing God made was the *Logos*, after which the *Logos* created everything else. So the *Logos* is higher than human beings and even angels. He is the Creator, and He predates all things except God. But He is not eternal, because He Himself was created by God, so He is not equal with God.

In time, according to adoptionism, the *Logos* became incarnate in the person of Jesus. In His human nature, the *Logos* was one with the Father in terms of carrying out the same mission and working toward the same goals. He was obedient to the Father, and because of His obedience, the Father "adopted" Him. Thus, it is proper to call the *Logos* the Son of God. However, He became the Son of God dynamically. There was a change. He was not always the Son of God, but His Sonship was something He earned.

Those who defended this view cited such biblical statements as "He is the image of the invisible God, the firstborn of all creation" (Col. 1:15). They also argued that the New Testament's descriptions of Christ as "begotten" carry the implication that He had a beginning in time, and anything that has a beginning in time is less than God, because God has no beginning. In short, they believed the *Logos* is like God, but He is not God.

These views prompted the first of the ecumenical councils, the Council of Nicea, which met in AD 325. This council produced the Nicene Creed, which affirms that Christ is "the only begotten Son of God, begotten of the Father before all worlds," and that He was "begotten, not made." It further declares that He is "God of God, Light of Light, very God of very God . . . being of one substance with the Father." With these affirmations, the church said that scriptural terms such as *firstborn* and *begotten* have to do with Christ's place of honor, not with His biological origin. The church declared that Christ is of the same substance, being, and essence as the Father. Thus, the idea was put forth that God, though three in person, is one in essence.

MONOPHYSITISM AND NESTORIANISM

The Council of Nicea represented a watershed moment for the church. For the most part, it put an end to monarchianism, but two new errors with respect to the nature of Christ soon developed.

The first was taught by a man named Eutyches. He was the first to articulate the monophysite heresy, which seems to appear anew in every generation. The term *mono-*

CONTROVERSIES IN THE EARLY CHURCH

physite consists of the now-familiar prefix *mono*, meaning "one," and *physite*, which comes from the Greek *phusis*, meaning "nature." So the word *monophysite* literally means "one nature."

Throughout the ages, the church has said that God is one in essence, being, or nature, and three in person. It has said just the opposite with respect to the person of Christ, who is said to be one person with two natures— one human and one divine. But Eutyches denied this truth. The monophysite heresy taught that Jesus had only one nature. Eutyches viewed Jesus as having one "theanthropic" nature. The word *theanthropic* comes from the Greek *anthropos*, which means "man or mankind," and the prefix *thea*, which means "God." So *theanthropic* is something of a mongrelized term that combines Greek words for God and for man. Eutyches was saying that in Christ there is only one nature—a divinely human nature, or, to express it the other way around, a humanly divine nature. But Eutyches' view was manifestly a denial that Christ had two natures, one human and the other divine. In fact, the monophysite heresy sees Christ as neither God nor man, but as something more than man and less than God. He represents a kind of deified humanity or a humanized deity. So the distinction between humanness and deity was obscured in this thinking.

But not only did the church have to fight against Eutyches and his monophysite heresy, it had to resist the twin heresy of Nestorianism, named after its founder, Nestorius. Nestorius basically said that one person cannot have two natures; if there are two natures, there must be two persons. Therefore, since Christ had both a divine nature and a human nature, He was a divine person and a human person co-existing. This was the opposite of the monophysite distortion. In the Nestorian heresy, the two natures of Christ were not merely distinguished, they were totally separated.

It is the prerogative of the theologian to make fine distinctions; that is what theology is about. Therefore, I tell my students, "One of the most important distinctions you will ever learn to make is the one between a distinction and a separation." We say that a human being is a duality—he has a physical dimension and a non-physical dimension, which the Bible describes in terms of body and soul. If I distinguish a person's body from his soul, I do no harm to him, but if I separate his body from his soul, I not only harm him, I kill him. By not grasping the difference between distinguishing and separating, Nestorius essentially destroyed the biblical Christ.

This truth is useful at many points in biblical interpretation. For instance, Jesus sometimes said that there were things He did not know. Theologians interpret those statements as evidence that Jesus' human nature is not omniscient. Of course, His divine nature is omniscient, so when Jesus spoke of something He did not know, He was manifesting the limitations of His human nature. Likewise, it's clear that Jesus perspired, became hungry, and had His side pierced, but we do not believe that the divine nature perspired, became hungry, or had its side pierced, because the Lord's divine nature does not have a body. Those were all manifestations of His humanity. Jesus has two natures, a divine nature and a human nature, and at times He reveals His human side, while at other times He reveals His divine side. We can distinguish the two without separating them. But when the human nature perspires, it is still united to a divine nature that does not perspire.

In church history, some have argued that there is a "communication" of divine attributes to the human nature. This, they have claimed, made it possible for the human body of Christ to be at more than one place at the same time. Spatial locality has always been understood as one of the limitations of humanity; a human nature cannot be in three places at the same time. However, a human nature can be joined to a divine nature, which *can* be in three places at the same time. The divine nature could be in Pittsburgh, Boston, and Washington at the same time. But the argument, historically, was about whether the physical body of Jesus, which belongs to His humanity, could be at three places at the same time, and some said it could because His divine nature communicates the divine attribute of omnipresence to His human nature. Well, it is one thing for the divine nature to communicate information to the human nature; however, it is another thing entirely for the divine nature to communicate attributes to the human nature because such a communication would deify the human nature.

This truth of the separation of Christ's natures was very important at the cross. The human nature died, but the divine nature did not die. Of course, at death, the divine nature was united to a human corpse. The unity was still there, but the change that had taken place was within the human nature, not the divine nature. That's very important to understand.

THE COUNCIL OF CHALCEDON

The Council of Chalcedon met in AD 451 to deal with the heresies of monophysitism and Nestorianism. Some scholars have argued that in the whole history of the church, Chalcedon was the terminal council as to Christology, meaning that the church has never really been able to go beyond the understanding of the person of Christ that was articulated at this council. I agree with that. It's possible, theoretically, that another council could be held in the twenty-first century, the twenty-second century, or the thirtieth century that might give us a new insight about the nature of Christ that we do not have now, but I have seen nothing in church history that goes beyond or improves upon the boundaries that were established for our reflection at the Council of Chalcedon.

The Council of Chalcedon produced the following statement, known as the Chalcedonian Creed:

> Therefore, following the holy fathers, we all with one accord teach men to acknowledge one and the same Son, our Lord Jesus Christ, at once complete in Godhead and complete in manhood, truly God and truly

man, consisting also of a reasonable soul and body; of one substance with the Father as regards his Godhead, and at the same time of one substance with us as regards his manhood; like us in all respects, apart from sin; as regards his Godhead, begotten of the Father before the ages, but yet as regards his manhood begotten, for us men and for our salvation, of Mary the Virgin, the God-bearer; one and the same Christ, Son, Lord, Only-begotten, recognized in two natures, without confusion, without change, without division, without separation; the distinction of natures being in no way annulled by the union, but rather the characteristics of each nature being preserved and coming together to form one person and subsistence, not as parted or separated into two persons, but one and the same Son and Only-begotten God the Word, Lord Jesus Christ; even as the prophets from earliest times spoke of him, and our Lord Jesus Christ himself taught us, and the creed of the fathers has handed down to us.

This creed is noteworthy for several reasons. First, it affirms that Christ is "truly God and truly man" (*Vera*

Deus, vera homo). This affirmation means that Jesus Christ, in the unity of His two natures, is both God and man. He has both a true divine nature and a true human nature.

Unfortunately, many people who should know better say that Chalcedon affirmed that Jesus was *fully* God and *fully* man. That is a contradiction. If we say that His person is completely and totally divine, then He must have only one nature. We cannot have a person who is completely divine *and* completely human at the same time and in the same relationship. That is an absurd idea.

In reality, Chalcedon affirmed that Jesus has two natures, one of which is divine. His divine nature is fully divine; it's not just semi-divine, it is completely divine. The divine nature of Christ possesses all of the attributes of deity, lacking none of them. At the same time, the human nature of Christ is fully human in terms of created humanity. The one thing we have that Jesus' human nature does not have is original sin. He is like us in all respects except sin. He is as human as Adam was in creation. All of the strengths and limitations of humanity are found in the human nature of Jesus.

Second, Chalcedon is known, perhaps most famously, for the so-called "four negatives." When the council confessed that there is a perfect unity between the divine and human natures in Christ, it said they are united in such a way as to be "without confusion, without change, without division, without separation." In other words, the council said that we cannot mix up the two natures of Christ; that was the heresy of the monophysites. Neither can we separate them; that was the error of the Nestorians. No, Jesus' two natures are perfectly united. We can distinguish them, but we cannot mix or divide them. We cannot conceive of the human and divine natures in Him as being confused or changed, so that we end up with a deified human nature or a humanized divine nature.

As you can see, we have to walk a razor's edge between confusion and separation if we are to gain a sound understanding of the person of Christ. I believe that some of the greatest minds in church history, including two of my all-time favorite theologians, were fundamentally monophysite in their understanding of Christ; at least they had monophysite elements in their thinking. I'm talking about Thomas Aquinas and Martin Luther. I have Lutheran friends, and I always refer to them as "my monophysite friends." They refer to me as their "Nestorian friend," but

I always say, "No, I don't separate the two natures, I just distinguish them."

Third, the Chalcedonian Creed affirms that the distinction of Jesus' two natures is "in no way annulled by the union, but rather the characteristics of each nature [are] preserved and [come] together to form one person and subsistence." In other words, in the incarnation, God does not give up any of His attributes and humanity does not give up any of its attributes. When Jesus came to earth, He did not lay aside His divine nature. Neither did He assume a human nature that was anything less than fully human. In the midst of controversy, the men of God who gathered at Chalcedon affirmed these things, and we should be eternally grateful.

It has been said that there have been four centuries when the church's understanding of the person of Christ has been most under attack. Those centuries were the fourth and fifth, as well as the nineteenth and twentieth. If this is true, we are living in the immediate aftermath of two hundred years of devastating attacks against the church's orthodox understanding of the person of Christ. That's why it's so important in our day that we revisit this whole concept of the Trinity.

Chapter Four

ONE IN ESSENCE, THREE IN PERSON

The New Testament epistle to the Hebrews begins with stirring words about the Lord Jesus Christ and His importance in God's unfolding revelation. We read:

Long ago, at many times and in many ways, God spoke to our fathers by the prophets, but in these last days he has spoken to us by his Son, whom he appointed the heir of all things, through whom also he created the world. He is the radiance of the glory of God and the exact imprint of his nature, and he upholds the universe by the word of his power. After making purification for sins, he sat down at the right hand of the Majesty on high, having become as much superior to angels as the name he has inherited is more excellent than theirs. (1:1–4)

The Christology that we find in the book of Hebrews is exceedingly high; in fact, it is one of the chief reasons why the early church was inclined to affirm the deity of Christ. Here we see Christ again described as the Son of God and as the agent of creation, who presents a vastly superior revelation than did the prophets of the Old Testament.

But the author also presents the concept that the Son of God is "the radiance of the glory of God and the exact imprint of his nature." This is a clear reference to Jesus' deity, but the author is also distinguishing the Son of God from the Father in terms of the idea of personhood. The Father's person is expressed in the person of the Son. So even though both the Father and Son are divine, the author of Hebrews here sets forth the idea of a personal distinction in the Godhead.

THE WORD *PERSON*

The use of the word *person* to distinguish the Father, Son, and Holy Ghost from one another can be problematic. The early church used the word *person* in a somewhat different manner than it is used today. That's a common problem with language—it is dynamic. Its nuances change from one generation to the next. In Elizabethan English, for example, if you called a girl "cute," you insulted her, because *cute* meant "bowlegged," whereas today it means something quite different.

The church father Tertullian, who had a background not only in theology but in law, introduced the Latin term *persona* in an attempt to express the *Logos* Christology of the early years of the church era. In the Latin language, this word was primarily used in relation to two concepts. First, it could refer to a person's possessions or estate. Second, it could refer to the dramatic stage presentations of the period. Sometimes actors had multiple roles in a play. Whenever an actor changed his role during the play, he would put on a different mask and assume a different persona.

In the late 1950s, there was a hit play on Broadway that was based on the biblical book of Job. It was titled *J.B.*

Basil Rathbone, who was famous for playing the role of Sherlock Holmes in a series of films, played both the role of God and the role of Satan in the Broadway production of *J.B.* I was fortunate enough to sit in the center of the front row, and Rathbone stood about five feet away from me. During the play, he had two masks, and when he was articulating the role of God, he would put on one mask, and when he was articulating the role of Satan, he would wear the other.

That dramatic technique was a throwback to the use of such masks in antiquity. The common symbol of stagecraft is two masks, one frowning, which represents dramatic tragedy, and one smiling, which represents comedy. Such masks actually were commonly used on stage by actors in antiquity to convey their roles, just as Rathbone used them in *J.B.* Each role was a *persona* and collectively they were *personae*. So the early church came to see God as one being with three personae: the Father, the Son, and the Holy Spirit.

THE WORD *ESSENCE*

As the church developed in its understanding of God during its first five centuries, other terms came into use, including *essence*, *existence*, and *subsistence*. To understand the import of these concepts, we have to go back into Greek thinking.

The province of the ancient philosophers was metaphysics, a form of physics that goes above and beyond what we perceive in this world. The Greek philosophers were looking for ultimate reality, that which does not manifest change. They were looking for the essence of things. They called it the *ousios*, which is the present participle of the Greek verb "to be." We would translate *ousios* into English by the word *being*. The best synonym for the Greek idea of being may be the English word *essence*.

Two philosophers who lived before Plato locked horns over the nature of reality. Parmenides, who was considered the most brilliant pre-Socratic philosopher, is famous for his statement, "Whatever is, is." He meant that for anything to be real ultimately, it has to be in a state of *being*; it has to have a real essence. If it does not, it is just a figment of our imaginations.

Parmenides' counterpart was Heraclitus. Some call him the father of modern existentialism. He said, "Whatever is, is changing." He believed that all things are in a state of flux. The only thing that is constant is change itself.

He said, "You can't step into the same river twice." He meant that if you step into a river and then step out, by the time you step in once again the river has moved on. It's not the same river that you stepped into the first time; it has gone through many minute changes. In fact, you're not the same person; you, too, have changed, if only by aging a few seconds. So Heraclitus said that what is most basic to all the reality that we perceive in this world is that everything is in a process of change. In other words, it is in a process of *becoming*.

When Plato arrived on the scene, he made an important distinction between being and becoming. He said that nothing can become anything unless it first participates in some way in being. If something were pure becoming, it would be only potentially something. Something that is mere potential would be nothing. Plato said that for becoming to be meaningful, there has to be some prior being.

In discussing the difference between being and becoming, Plato spoke of the difference between essence (which is the *being* element of something, the substance of it) and existence (which is the *becoming* element).

THE WORDS *EXISTENCE* AND *SUBSISTENCE*

The word *existence* is derived from the prefix *ex*, which means "out of," and the root *sisto*, a Greek verb meaning "to stand." So "to exist" literally means "to stand out of something." It is describing a position or a posture. The idea, I think, is that a person has one foot in being and the other foot in non-being. So he is standing out of being, but he is also standing out of non-being. He's between pure being and nothingness. That is the realm of becoming or existence. Thus, when the church articulated the doctrine of the Trinity, it did not say that God is one in essence and three in existences. Instead, it said three in person.

I once gave a lecture in which I publicly denied the existence of God. I said: "I want to emphatically affirm today that God does not exist. In fact, if He did exist, I would stop believing in Him." If anything ever sounded like a nonsense statement, that was it. But I simply meant that God is not in a state of becoming. He is in a state of pure being. If He were in a state of existence, He would be changing—at least according to the way this term is used in philosophy. He would not be immutable. He would not be the God we believe in.

When Plato dealt with these concepts, there were basically three categories: being, becoming, and non-being. Non-being, of course, is a synonym for nothing. What is nothing? To ask that question is to answer it. If I say nothing is something, I am attributing something to nothing. I'm saying nothing has some content, that nothing has being. But if it has being, it is not nothing, it is something. As you can see, one of the most difficult concepts to deal with in philosophy is the concept of pure nothingness. Try to think about pure nothingness—you can't do it. The closest I ever came to a definition of nothingness was when my son was in junior high. He would come home from school and I would say, "What did you do in school today?" He would say, "Nothing." So I began to think that I might be able to define nothing as what my son did in school everyday. But in reality, it's impossible to do nothing. If you're doing, you're doing something.

The word *person* is equivalent to the term *subsistence*. In this word, we have the prefix *sub* with the same root word, *sisto*, so *subsistence* literally means "to stand under." Thus, this word gets at the idea that while God is one in essence, there are three subsistences, three persons, that stand under the essence. They are part of the essence. All three have the essence of deity.

Nevertheless, we can make a distinction between the three persons of the Trinity, because each member of the Godhead has unique attributes. We say the Father is God, the Son is God, and the Holy Spirit is God, but we don't say that the Father is the Son, the Son is the Holy Spirit, or the Holy Spirit is the Father. There are distinctions between them, but the distinctions are not essential, not of the essence. They are real, but they do not disturb the essence of deity. The distinctions within the Godhead are, if you will, sub-distinctions within the essence of God. He is one essence, three subsistences. That is about as close as we can get to articulating the historic doctrine of the Trinity.

Chapter Five

OBJECTIONS
TO THE DOCTRINE

Perhaps the most consistent objection to the doctrine of the Trinity is that it is irrational because it involves a contradiction. As I noted in chapter one, calling the Trinity a contradiction is a misapplication of the law of non-contradiction. The doctrine of the Trinity teaches that God is one in essence and three in person, so He is one in one sense and three in another sense, and that does not violate the categories of rational thought or the law of non-contradiction. Nevertheless, people continue to charge that the Trinity is irrational. Why do people so consistently make this accusation?

There are three distinct ideas that we need to understand and differentiate: the paradox, the contradiction, and the mystery. Although these concepts are distinctly different, they are closely related. For this reason, they are often confused.

Let's start with the concept of paradox. The prefix *para* means "alongside." The root word here comes from the Greek *dokeo*, which means "to seem, to think, or to appear." A paradox, then, is something that seems contradictory when we first encounter it; however, with further scrutiny, the tension is resolved. The Bible has many paradoxical statements. For instance, Jesus said, "The greatest among you shall be your servant" (Matt. 23:11). At first glance, that sounds contradictory, but on closer examination we see that Jesus is saying that to be great in one sense you have to be a servant in another sense, so there is no violation here of the rules of logic.

The real tension occurs when we encounter mysteries and contradictions. We use the term *mystery* to refer to things we do not yet understand. We may believe a mystery is true, but we do not understand why it is true. For instance, we know that there is such a thing as gravity, but the essence of gravity remains something of a mystery to us. Even something as basic as motion, which we notice and utilize every day, defies an acute analysis. When we look at it philosophically, we have to say that there is a mysterious element to motion, and the same is true for many other things that we experience in our everyday lives.

UNRAVELING MYSTERIES

Sometimes, as we get new information, things that once seemed mysterious to us are unraveled. We have seen real progress in knowledge in the history of science and other disciplines. But even if we increase our knowledge to the maximum point in human experience, we will always remain finite creatures who will not have the ability to comprehend all reality.

There are many truths that God reveals to us about Himself that are beyond our capacity to understand. Given the difference between the exalted character of God and our status as created beings, this difficulty should not surprise us. We may come to greater understanding of many of these mysterious truths at some future point in redemptive history. However, even then we may never fully understand some truths.

So, something is a mystery to us if we lack understanding of it; this is quite different from a contradiction. Yet, no one understands a contradiction either. It is this similarity that leads to the idea that the Trinity is a contradiction. We can rush to judgment and say, "If we don't understand something, it must be irrational, it must be a contradiction." But that's not necessarily the case. It is true that contradictions cannot be understood because they are inherently unintelligible, but not everything that seems to be a contradiction is a contradiction. Some apparent contradictions are mysteries.

In my seminary days, I once heard a professor say, with a wrinkled brow and a hushed tone, "God is absolutely immutable in His essence and absolutely mutable in His essence." There was a collective sigh by the students, as if they all were thinking, "That's deep." I wanted to say, "No, that's nuts, that's wacky." But if you have enough education and a position of authority in the academic world, you can make nonsense statements and people will walk away impressed by how profound you seem. But it is profoundly nonsensical to say that God is absolutely immutable and absolutely mutable at the same time and in the same relationship. Even someone with all the degrees in the world could not make sense of that statement. That statement is a true contradiction.

CAN GOD UNDERSTAND CONTRADICTIONS?

Some people actually say that the difference between God and man is that whereas our minds are limited by the laws of logic, God's mind transcends the laws of logic, so He can understand something as A and non-A at the same time and in the same relationship. I suppose they believe they are exalting God by saying that He is so wonderful in His intelligence and so transcendent in His wisdom as to be able to understand contradictions. Actually, those who say this kind of thing slander Him, because they are saying that nonsense and chaos reside in the mind of God, which is not the case.

It is true that there are things that we do not understand, things that are mysterious to us, that God can readily understand from His perspective and with His omniscience. For God, there are no mysteries. He understands gravity, motion, and ultimate reality and being. Likewise, there are no contradictions for Him, for His understanding is perfectly consistent.

The fact that Christ has two natures is certainly a mystery to us. We cannot grasp how a person can have both a divine nature and a human nature. We have no reference point for that in our human experience. Every person we have ever met has had only one nature. When we affirm the dual natures of Christ, we are affirming something that is unique to Him, something that differs from the normal experience of humanity. It's difficult to even describe. As we saw in the previous chapter, the Council of Chalcedon declared that the divine and human natures in Christ are "without confusion, without change, without division, without separation." But those affirmations are merely saying how the two natures in Christ do *not* relate. We cannot really say how His two natures function together.

Likewise, when we come to the doctrine of the Trinity, we say, based on the revelation of Scripture, that there is a sense in which God is one and another sense in which He is three. We must be careful to point out that those two senses are not the same. If they were the same, we would be espousing a contradiction unworthy of our faith. But they are different, and so the doctrine of the Trinity is not

a contradiction but a mystery, for we cannot fully understand how one God can exist in three persons.

THE USE OF THE WORD *TRINITY*

Another objection that frequently is raised against the doctrine of the Trinity is that the Bible, and particularly the
New Testament, never uses the term *Trinity*. It is an extra-
biblical word. Sometimes it is said that it is a term imposed
on the text of Scripture, and therefore it involves an intru-
sion into the Hebraic mind of the Scriptures from outside
the biblical framework. It is said to represent an invasion of
abstract Greek categories into New Testament Christianity.
We hear these kinds of comments all the time, as if the
Holy Spirit could not use the Greek language as a medium
of communicating truth, which we know is not the case,
since much of the New Testament was written in the Greek
language. So theologians and philosophers sometimes have
more trouble with Greek than God does.

But the question we must ask is this: Does the concept that is represented by the word *Trinity* appear in the
Bible? All that the word *Trinity* does is capture linguisti-
cally the scriptural teaching on the unity of God and the

tri-personality of God. Seeing these concepts in Scripture, we search for a word that accurately communicates them. We come up with the idea of "tri-unity," three in oneness, and so we coin this term *Trinity*. It really is naive to object that the word itself is not found in Scripture if the concept is found in Scripture and is taught by Scripture.

Theological terms such as *Trinity* have arisen in church history principally because of the church's commitment to theological precision. John Calvin made the observation in his *Institutes of the Christian Religion* that words such as *Trinity* have come about because of what he described as the "slippery snakes" who try to distort the teaching of Scripture by heresy.[1] The favorite trick of the heretic is what we call studied ambiguity—that means of communication whereby concepts are intentionally left ambiguous. Theological precision is necessary to combat this tactic.

The Protestant Reformation of the sixteenth century was a contrast between studied ambiguity and theological precision. The basic issue of the Reformation concerned the grounds of our justification. Is our justification grounded

---

1 John Calvin, *Institutes of the Christian Religion*, ed. John T. McNeill, trans. Ford Lewis Battles, Library of Christian Classics, Vols. XX–XXI (Philadelphia: Westminster John Knox, 1960), 1.13.4.

in a righteousness that inheres within us or in a righteousness that is imputed to us? That is, is our righteousness from within us or from Christ? The controversy came down to one word: *imputation*. The Reformers objected to the Roman Catholic teaching, saying the only way any person can be justified is to have the righteousness of Jesus Christ imputed, or transferred, to his account.

Attempting to resolve the dispute, many people suggested that the two sides should simply say, "We are justified by Christ." They said that since Roman Catholics and Protestants agreed that people are justified by Christ, everyone could hold hands, sing hymns, pray together, and stay together. This proposed statement was so ambiguous that people who believe we are justified by the infusion of the righteousness of Jesus and people who believe we are justified by the imputation of the righteousness of Jesus could agree to it. However, these two views of justification are as far from each other as the east is from the west. The idea was that the controversy could be avoided and division healed by using a formula that was intentionally ambiguous, a statement that could be interpreted in radically different ways. So the Protestants insisted on the term *imputation*, even at the cost of division.

A VALUABLE SHIBBOLETH

In like manner, the church has used the term *Trinity* to stop the mouths of the heretics, those who teach tritheism (the idea that there are three Gods) and those who deny the tri-personality of God by insisting on some view of unitarianism. We might say that the word *Trinity* is a "shibboleth." The book of Judges tells of the conflict between the men of Gilead, led by Jephthah, and the men of Ephraim. To identify their enemies, the soldiers of Gilead required strangers to say "Shibboleth." The Ephraimites could not pronounce that word, and that inability gave them away (Judg. 12:5–6). That password has become a term for a test word by which someone's true identity can be ascertained.

In Holland, during the period of the German occupation during World War II, the people also had a shibboleth. There is a resort town on the coast of Holland called Scheveningen. The Germans simply could not say it properly. They could speak Dutch and pass as Dutch people under most circumstances, but if they were asked to say the word *Scheveningen*, they stumbled. That word became a shibboleth that helped the Dutch identify spies.

The church should not hesitate to use certain words as shibboleths to force people to reveal where they stand on various issues. J. I. Packer has identified one such shibboleth: *inerrancy*. If you want to find out where a person stands with respect to sacred Scripture, you should not ask him whether he believes in the inspiration of the Scriptures. You should ask, "Do you believe in the inerrancy of Scripture?" because many people will choke on that word before they will affirm it.

Trinity is a perfectly good word that accurately states that which the church has believed and confessed historically. We should not hesitate to use it and other such words to set the standard of truth as accurately as possible.

Further your Bible study with *Tabletalk* magazine, another learning tool from R.C. Sproul.

....

Sign up for a free 3-month trial of *Tabletalk* magazine and we will send you R.C. Sproul's *The Holiness of God*

TryTabletalk.com/CQ

About the Author

Dr. R.C. Sproul is the founder and chairman of Ligonier Ministries, an international Christian discipleship organization located near Orlando, Fla. He also serves as copastor at Saint Andrew's Chapel in Sanford, Fla., as chancellor of Reformation Bible College, and as executive editor of *Tabletalk* magazine. His teaching can be heard around the world on the daily radio program *Renewing Your Mind*.

During his distinguished academic career, Dr. Sproul helped train men for the ministry as a professor at several theological seminaries.

He is author of more than ninety books, including *The Holiness of God, Chosen by God, The Invisible Hand, Faith Alone, Everyone's a Theologian, Truths We Confess, The Truth of the Cross*, and *The Prayer of the Lord*. He also served as general editor of the *Reformation Study Bible* and has written several children's books, including *The Donkey Who Carried a King*. Dr. Sproul and his wife, Vesta, make their home in Sanford, Fla.